General Assembly
Official Records
Seventieth Session
Supplement No. 48

Report of the Committee on the Protection of the Rights of All Migrant Workers and Members of Their Families

Twenty-first session
(1-5 September 2014)

Twenty-second session
(13-24 April 2015)

United Nations • New York, 2015

Note

Symbols of United Nations documents are composed of letters combined with figures. Mention of such a symbol indicates a reference to a United Nations document.

ISSN

[19 August 2015]

Contents

Chapter		Paragraphs	Page
I.	Organizational and other matters		4
	A. States parties to the Convention		4
	B. Meetings and sessions		4
	C. Membership and attendance		4
	D. Future meetings of the Committee		4
	E. Participation in the twenty-sixth meeting of the Chairs of the human rights treaty bodies		5
	F. General comments and general discussion days		5
	G. Promotion of the Convention		5
	H. Meeting with States parties		9
	I. Adoption of the report		9
II.	Methods of work		9
III.	Cooperation with bodies concerned		10
IV.	Reports of States parties under article 73 of the Convention		11
V.	Consideration of reports submitted by States parties in accordance with article 74 of the Convention		11
	A. Adoption of lists of issues and lists of issues prior to reporting		11
	B. Adoption of concluding observations		12

Annexes

I.	States that have signed, ratified or acceded to the International Convention on the Protection of the Rights of All Migrant Workers and Members of Their Families as at 24 April 2015	13
II.	Membership of the Committee on the Protection of the Rights of All Migrant Workers and Members of Their Families as at 24 April 2015	16
III.	Submission of reports under article 73 of the Convention as at 24 April 2015	17
IV.	List of documents issued or to be issued in connection with the twenty-first and twenty-second sessions of the Committee	22

I. Organizational and other matters

A. States parties to the Convention

1. On 24 April 2015, the closing date of the twenty-second session of the Committee on the Protection of the Rights of All Migrant Workers and Members of Their Families (the Committee), there were 47 States parties to the International Convention on the Protection of the Rights of All Migrant Workers and Members of Their Families (the Convention). The Convention was adopted by the General Assembly in resolution 45/158 on 18 December 1990 and entered into force on 1 July 2003, in accordance with the provisions of its article 87 (1).

2. A list of States that have signed, ratified or acceded to the Convention is contained in annex I. The updated status of the Convention, together with the texts of declarations and reservations and other relevant information, can be found in the United Nations Treaty Collection online at http://treaties.un.org, which is maintained by the Treaty Section of the Office of Legal Affairs, which discharges the depositary functions of the Secretary-General.

B. Meetings and sessions

3. The Committee held its twenty-first session at the United Nations Office at Geneva from 1 to 5 September 2014, consisting of 10 plenary meetings (see CMW/C/SR.262-271). The provisional agenda, contained in document CMW/C/21/1, was adopted by the Committee at its 262nd meeting, on 1 September 2014.

4. The Committee held its twenty-second session at the United Nations Office at Geneva from 13 to 24 April 2015, consisting of 19 plenary meetings (see CMW/C/SR.272-290). The provisional agenda, contained in document CMW/C/22/1, was adopted by the Committee at its 272nd meeting, on 13 April 2015.

C. Membership and attendance

5. All the members of the Committee attended its twenty-first session, except for Md. Shahidul Haque. Abdelhamid El Jamri and Marco Nuñez-Melgar Maguiña were absent on the first day of the session.

6. All the members of the Committee attended its twenty-second session, except for Abdelhamid El-Jamri. Md. Shahidul Haque was absent for the second week of the session, and Ahmed Hassan El-Borai was absent on the last day of the session.

7. The list of the members of the Committee as at 24 April 2015, together with the duration of their terms of office, is provided in annex II to the present report.

D. Future meetings of the Committee

8. The twenty-third session of the Committee will be held from 31 August to 9 September 2015 at the United Nations Office at Geneva. The Committee was granted three additional days of meeting time following the adoption of General Assembly resolution 68/268 on strengthening and enhancing the effective functioning of the human rights treaty body system. That extra time will allow the Committee to review additional reports of States parties annually.

9. The twenty-fourth session of the Committee will be held for a two-week period in April 2016 at the United Nations Office at Geneva. The dates have not yet been confirmed.

E. Participation in the twenty-sixth meeting of the Chairs of the human rights treaty bodies

10. The Chair of the Committee, Francisco Carrión Mena, participated in the twenty-sixth meeting of the Chairs of the human rights treaty bodies, held in Geneva from 23 to 27 June 2014 (see A/69/285). The Chairs discussed the implementation of General Assembly resolution 68/268 with respect to three distinct areas, namely, the simplified reporting procedure, the alignment of methodologies for the constructive dialogues with States parties and a common format for short, focused and actionable concluding observations. The reports of and information on the annual meetings of the Chairs of the human rights treaty bodies may be found on the webpage of the annual meeting of Chairs of human rights treaty bodies.[1]

11. The Chair of the Committee also participated in an informal meeting of the Chairs of the human rights treaty bodies, along with representatives of Governments and civil society, held in Wilton Park (United Kingdom of Great Britain and Northern Ireland) from 14 to 16 January 2015. The meeting focused on the recent developments in strengthening United Nations human rights monitoring. In particular, discussions took place on how to achieve greater compliance by States with their reporting and human rights obligations under the treaties. The Chairs issued a joint statement on the post-2015 development agenda, highlighting that development efforts previously excluded the marginalized and disempowered and urging Member States to maintain and strengthen consistent alignment with and references to human rights. The statement and additional information on the meeting may be found on the webpage of the annual meeting of Chairs of human rights treaty bodies.[2]

F. General comments and general discussion days

12. The Committee decided, at its twenty-first session, that it would develop a general comment on the human rights of children in the context of migration. The Committee met with the Committee on the Rights of the Child on 3 September 2014 to discuss the possibility of a joint general comment in that regard. During its twenty-second session, the Committee met with United Nations agencies and civil society partners to discuss a concept note on the scope, content and time frame of the general comment, as well as opportunities for future consultations. All the participants in that meeting expressed support for the initiative and their readiness to contribute to its development.

G. Promotion of the Convention

13. In July 2014, the Chair of the Committee issued a statement on ending immigration detention of children,[3] in which he called upon States to adopt alternatives to detention in order to fulfil the best interests of the child and to allow children to remain with their families while their immigration status is being resolved. The Chair also called upon States to respect their obligations under the core United

---

[1] See www.ohchr.org/EN/HRBodies/AnnualMeeting/Pages/MeetingChairpersons.aspx.
[2] Ibid.
[3] See www.ohchr.org/EN/NewsEvents/pages/DisplayNews.aspx?NewsID=14825&LangID=E.

Nations human rights treaties that they have ratified and to ratify those treaties to which they are not yet party.

14. During its twenty-second session, the Committee issued two press releases entitled, "Latest migrant tragedy highlights shared responsibility of all countries"[4] and "Cooperate to save migrants' lives",[5] and one statement entitled, "Another human rights tragedy in the Mediterranean".[6] In those releases, the Committee stated that the loss of life in the Mediterranean Sea demanded that States adopt a new approach to migration that places the human rights of migrants at the forefront as well as addresses the root causes of this very complex phenomenon of cooperation with States of origin, transit and destination. The Committee also called upon States to ratify the Convention as it represents the best strategy to prevent abuses and address the vulnerabilities that migrant workers face, as well as provides guidance on the designing of national migration policies for international cooperation based on respect for human rights and the rule of law.

15. Members of the Committee continued to promote the Convention and the human rights of migrant workers and members of their families by (a) participating in conferences, meetings, workshops and side events of United Nations agencies and offices, including the Office of the United Nations High Commissioner for Human Rights (OHCHR), the International Labour Organization (ILO) and other international organizations, such as the International Organization for Migration (IOM), and civil society organizations; (b) advising States parties on treaty implementation and the reporting process; (c) contributing to publications on the human rights of migrant workers and other migration-related issues; and (d) participating in various fora with academia, students and other stakeholders.

16. The following Committee members reported on their activities at the twenty-first and twenty-second sessions: Mr. Carrión Mena (Chair), Ms. Castellanos Delgado, Mr. Ceriani Cernadas, Ms. Dicko, Mr. El-Borai, Mr. Haque, Ms. Ladjel, Mr. Nuñez-Melgar Maguiña, Mr. Pimé, Mr. Taghizada, and Mr. Tall.

17. During its twenty-first and twenty-second sessions, the Committee met the Director of OHCHR Human Rights Treaties Division and the Chief of the Groups in Focus Section to discuss ways to promote the Convention through, inter alia, personal advocacy on the part of the High Commissioner and other mechanisms, including the treaty bodies, special procedures mandate holders and the universal periodic review; strengthening engagement with OHCHR field presences and partners, including international trade unions; increasing awareness-raising activities and publications; and making better use of the media.

18. The Committee also had the opportunity to meet with the Migration Advisor of OHCHR to discuss activities relating to the promotion of the Convention, including the organization of a side event on protection at international borders during the June 2014 session of the Human Rights Council as well as a side event on domestic migrant workers, which was co-organized with ILO and held during the twenty-first session of the Committee. The Committee met again with the Migration Adviser during the twenty-second session and was briefed on the latest activities undertaken by OHCHR in the area of migration, including the launch of two publications entitled, *Recommended Principles and Guidelines on Human Rights at International Borders* and *The Economic, Social and Cultural Rights of Migrants in an Irregular Situation*, and updates of the Global Migration Group and the Global Forum on Migration and Development.

---

[4] See www.ohchr.org/EN/NewsEvents/Pages/DisplayNews.aspx?NewsID=15853&LangID=E.
[5] See www.ohchr.org/EN/NewsEvents/Pages/DisplayNews.aspx?NewsID=15870&LangID=E.
[6] See www.ohchr.org/EN/NewsEvents/Pages/DisplayNews.aspx?NewsID=15852&LangID=E.

19. At its twenty-first session, the Committee sent a letter to the new High Commissioner for Human Rights, Zeid Ra'ad Al Hussein, congratulating him on his appointment and requesting a meeting with him at its next session in order to discuss ways to promote ratification of the Convention. It also decided to send letters to all States parties that had not yet made the declaration recognizing the competence of the Committee to consider individual communications under article 77 of the Convention. At its twenty-second session, the Committee sent another letter to the High Commissioner, who was unable to meet with it during that session, requesting a meeting with him at its twenty-third session. The Committee also sent letters to the High Commissioner, the Secretary-General and the European Union with a view to urging the international community to adopt the OHCHR *Recommended Principles and Guidelines on Human Rights at International Borders* and to mobilize in order to address the complex phenomenon of migration, including the root causes of irregular migration, and to find durable solutions that place the human rights of migrants at the forefront of cooperation with States of origin, transit and destination.

20. OHCHR and members of the Steering Committee of the Global Campaign for Ratification of the Convention on Rights of Migrants (the Steering Committee) also collaborated to promote the Convention at the Global Forum on Migration and Development, held in Stockholm from 14 to 16 May 2014. OHCHR, other agencies and civil society organizations highlighted the need for a human rights-based approach to the issue of migration and development based on international human rights norms. In his opening remarks to the Forum, the Secretary-General stressed the importance of promoting and protecting the human rights of all migrants and members of their families and advocated for a human rights-based approach to migration policies and practices as part of the post-2015 development agenda. He also called upon States to ratify the Convention.

21. On 24 October 2014, the Chair of the Committee presented the annual report on its nineteenth and twentieth sessions (A/69/48) to the Third Committee of the General Assembly. The Chair also took part in a joint press conference with the Special Rapporteur on the human rights of migrants, during which he highlighted the human rights abuses that migrant workers face, underscored the need for States to develop sound migration policies and promoted the ratification of the Convention. The Chair also issued a statement calling on States to decriminalize irregular migration noting that the legitimate interests of States in securing their borders and exercising immigration control cannot override their obligation to respect, protect and fulfil the human rights of all persons in all areas under their jurisdiction, regardless of their migration status.[7]

22. Members of the Committee attended the Second Global Forum on Human Rights, held in Marrakech, Morocco, from 27 to 30 November 2014, which was organized by the National Council for Human Rights of the Kingdom of Morocco. The Forum brought together over 6,000 participants representing local and international non-governmental organizations, United Nations agencies, Governments, national institutions, international organizations, professional associations, political leaders, trade unions and businesses. The Forum provided a platform to discuss several issues, including the rights of children, women, persons with disabilities and migrants, and provided an opportunity for Committee members to highlight the work of the Committee and promote ratification of the Convention. The Committee wishes to thank the National Council for Human Rights of the Kingdom of Morocco for the invitation and generous support, which enabled several members of the Committee to attend the Forum.

---

[7] See www.ohchr.org/EN/NewsEvents/Pages/DisplayNews.aspx?NewsID=15207&LangID=E.

23. OHCHR participated in the Migrant Workers' Rights Capacity Building Workshop, held in Dubai from 2 to 3 November 2014, which was organized by the Diplomacy Training Program (affiliated with the Faculty of Law of the University of New South Wales) and Migrant Forum in Asia. The workshop brought together civil society actors in the Asia-Pacific and the Middle East and North Africa regions. It was attended by 30 participants representing non-governmental organizations, trade unions, the media, ILO and OHCHR. The workshop covered a number of topics relating to discussions on challenges for migrant workers advocacy and implementation of human rights and labour rights, promotion of international standards and their implementation, effective engagement with United Nations mechanisms, future collaboration and networking, promotion of the ratification of the Convention and the 25th anniversary of its adoption, including discussions on the global campaign, Step It Up: Dignity. Rights. Development.

24. The Step It Up campaign was launched on 18 December 2014 by the Migrant Forum in Asia network and affiliated civil society organizations, trade unions, OHCHR and ILO to mark the 25th anniversary of the adoption of the Convention, which will take place on 18 December 2015. Activities relating to the promotion of the human rights of migrant workers and members of their families as well as engagements with States to ratify the Convention can be found on the online platform of the campaign (http://cmw25.org/).

25. To mark International Migrants Day on 18 December 2014, a joint statement entitled, "Open, safe and regular migration channels crucial to stop human rights violations against migrants" was issued by the Special Rapporteur on the human rights of migrants; the Chair of the Committee; the Special Rapporteur on Refugees, Asylum Seekers, Internally Displaced Persons and Migrants of the African Commission on Human and Peoples' Rights; and Rapporteur on the Rights of Migrants of the Inter-American Commission on Human Rights of the Organization of American States.[8]

26. OHCHR also organized two meetings of the Steering Committee of the Global Campaign for Ratification of the Convention on Rights of Migrants in June 2014 and February 2015. The Steering Committee is comprised of representatives of intergovernmental agencies and leading international human rights, church, labour, migrant and women's organizations. The discussions focused on ways and means to further promote ratification of the Convention as well as activities to mark the 25th anniversary of the adoption of the Convention.

27. Members of the Steering Committee also met with the Committee at its twenty-second session and briefed it on its activities relating to the promotion of the Convention as well as events to mark the 25th anniversary of the Convention. They also discussed the adverse migrant environment and challenges in that regard; the requirement of legislative, policy, practical and public relations efforts as well as the allocation of significant material, financial and human resources by Governments and stakeholders for the ratification, domestication and implementation of the Convention; the fact that a strategic, long-term approach is more essential than ever to achieve further ratifications; and the very positive developments in certain parts of the world with regard to civil society and trade union activism in relation to the human rights of migrant workers. Representatives from ILO, IOM, the International Trade Union Confederation and Global Migration Policy Associates also attended the meeting. The Committee also met with Professor Nicola Piper, Professor of International Migration, School of Social and Political Sciences, University of Sydney, who discussed a book containing country case studies on the implementation of the Convention and a research project on the negotiations leading up to the adoption of the Convention in 1990, and how that information could help promote ratification of the Convention.

---

[8] See www.ohchr.org/EN/NewsEvents/Pages/DisplayNews.aspx?NewsID=15438&LangID=E.

H. Meeting with States parties

28. The Chair of the Committee met with representatives of the Permanent Missions of Brazil, Norway and South Africa, in New York in October 2014, concerning the promotion of the ratification of the Convention. At its twenty-second session, the Committee held an informal meeting with States parties and briefed them on the status of the Convention and the activities of the Committee relating to the promotion of the ratification of the Convention, including the implementation of General Assembly resolution 68/268. The Chair also discussed ways and means to increase the number of ratifications of the Convention as well as the activities to mark the 25th anniversary of the adoption of the Convention. The Director of OHCHR Human Rights Treaties Division took the opportunity to brief States parties on the activities of the Office to promote ratification of the Convention, including urging signatory States to ratify it; liaising with civil society and international trade unions; following up recommendations made during the second cycle of the universal periodic review with both the States concerned and relevant OHCHR field presences; as well as the personal advocacy and commitment of the High Commissioner. The Chair also met with the Permanent Representative of Turkey during the twenty-second session.

I. Adoption of the report

29. On 24 April 2015, at the 290th meeting of the twenty-second session, the Committee adopted the present annual report to the General Assembly.

II. Methods of work

30. During its twenty-first session, the Committee met with the Chief of the Groups in Focus Section of OHCHR Human Rights Treaties Division with regard to the implementation of General Assembly resolution A/68/268. The Committee considered the guidance note on the constructive dialogue and the framework for the concluding observations, which is annexed to the report of the Chairs of the human rights treaty bodies on their 26th meeting (see A/69/285, annexes I and II). Although the Committee acknowledged that the guidelines broadly conformed to its working methods, it decided to postpone formal endorsement until the twenty-second session. The Committee pointed out in that regard that it was the first treaty body to adopt all the proposals and recommendations addressed to the treaty bodies in the report of the High Commissioner for Human Rights on strengthening the United Nations human rights treaty body system (see A/66/860, section 4), including those concerning independence and impartiality of members of the human rights bodies in the exercise of their functions and the simplified reporting procedure. It also mentioned that it raised priority concerns during the constructive dialogues with States parties and did not cover all the articles of the Convention. Consequently, time management is not an issue and the concluding observations focused on priority concerns. The Committee further indicated that dialogues with States parties started in the afternoon and concluded the following day, which allowed the State party to consult with authorities in the capital.

31. The Committee decided to strengthen the role of the Country Rapporteur by allowing time prior to the constructive dialogue with a State party for the Rapporteur to brief the Committee on priority concerns in the State party that it may wish to raise during the dialogue.

32. The Committee also decided to initiate a follow-up procedure, whereby it requests State parties to provide information on the implementation of priority recommendations highlighted in the concluding observations. It decided that the Country Rapporteurs would act as Rapporteurs for follow-up with regard to the State parties concerned.

33. During its twenty-second session, the Committee considered the guidance note on the constructive dialogue and the framework for the concluding observations, annexed to the report of the Chairs on their 26th meeting (see A/69/285, annexes I and II) and endorsed them, noting that its practice largely conformed to the guidelines. The Committee also discussed the issue of reprisals. In that regard, noting that it had not yet faced the issue and that the Chairs of the human rights treaty bodies would be adopting policy guidelines on reprisals at their 27th meeting, the Committee decided to not appoint a Rapporteur on the issue at that time, but to refer such matters to the Bureau for review, which in turn would make recommendations to the Committee for a decision.

34. The Committee discussed its practice with respect to the guidelines on the independence and impartiality of members of the human rights treaty bodies (Addis Ababa Guidelines) (see A/67/222, annex I) and considered a draft decision on incorporating the guidelines into its rules of procedure with modifications and additions. The Committee will discuss this further at its next session. The Committee further discussed establishing a long-term programme of work for its methods of work and general comments and decided to further discuss the matter at its next session; it requested Mr. Ceriani Cernadas and Ms. Ladjel to prepare a concept note in that regard. The Committee decided to accept the invitation of the Government of Azerbaijan to hold an informal meeting in Baku at the end of October 2015. It decided that it would take advantage of that opportunity to discuss a long-term programme of work, working methods and other matters, including its general comment on children in situations of migration. The Committee thanked the Government of Azerbaijan for its very invitation.

III. Cooperation with bodies concerned

35. The Committee continued its cooperation with United Nations specialized agencies, intergovernmental organizations and civil society organizations. While welcoming their contributions in relation to the consideration of the reports of States parties, the Committee encouraged them to cooperate more actively with it by submitting country-specific information.

36. The Committee adopted a statement on its relationship with civil society organizations with a view to clarifying and strengthening that relationship and enhancing the role of those organizations in the implementation of the Convention by States parties at the national level.[9]

37. The Committee continued close cooperation with ILO, which assists it in a consultative capacity, in accordance with article 74 (5) of the Convention.

38. The Committee continued its cooperation with the Special Rapporteur on the human rights of migrants. The Chair of the Committee and the Special Rapporteur issued a joint press statement and participated in a joint press conference to promote the ratification of the Convention and the human rights of migrant workers, in October 2014, when the Chair presented the annual report of the Committee to the Third Committee of the General Assembly.

---

[9] See statement on the Committee's webpage, available from www2.ohchr.org.

39. Furthermore, the Committee discussed possible joint initiatives with other treaty bodies on issues concerning the rights of migrant workers. In that regard, the Committee provided input to Human Rights Committee general comment on article 9 of the International Covenant on Civil and Political Rights on the right to liberty and security of person. The Committee also met with the Committee on the Rights of the Child, in September 2014, to explore the possibility of developing a joint general comment on the human rights of children in the context of migration.

40. During its twenty-second session, the Committee met with OHCHR Business and Human Rights Adviser, who briefed it on the Guiding Principles on Business and Human Rights. The ensuing discussion focused on the obligations of States to prevent, punish and provide redress for human rights abuses by businesses, as well as the human rights responsibilities of businesses. The Committee also discuss the challenges relating to complex mixed migration flows and the overlapping of boundaries between international understandings of refugees and "voluntary" migrants with representatives of the Human Rights Liaison Unit of the Office of the United Nations High Commissioner for Refugees. Those discussions will help the Committee to provide more targeted recommendations in their concluding observations on the reports of States parties.

IV. Reports of States parties under article 73 of the Convention

41. The Committee noted with concern that, as at 13 April 2015, initial and periodic reports due under article 73 of the Convention had not yet been received from as many as 22 States parties. Annex III contains a table showing the due dates of the reports of States parties.

V. Consideration of reports submitted by States parties in accordance with article 74 of the Convention

A. Adoption of lists of issues and lists of issues prior to reporting

42. At its twenty-first session, the Committee adopted a list of issues in relation to the following report:

State party	Type of report	Symbol of report	Symbol of list of issues
Peru	Initial	CMW/C/PER/1	CMW/C/PER/Q/1

43. At its twenty-first and twenty-second, the Committee adopted lists of issues prior to reporting in relation to States parties that had accepted to report under the optional simplified reporting procedure and those that had been notified, under rule 31 bis of the revised provisional rules of procedure (see A/67/48 and Corr.1, para. 26):

State party	Type of report (due since)	Symbol of list of issues prior to reporting
Honduras	Initial (1 December 2006)	CMW/C/HND/QPR/1
Lesotho	Initial (1 January 2007)	CMW/C/LSO/QPR/1
Mauritania	Initial (1 May 2008)	CMW/C/MRT/QPR/1
Nicaragua	Initial (1 February 2007)	CMW/C/NIC/QPR/1

State party	Type of report (due since)	Symbol of list of issues prior to reporting
Niger	Initial (1 July 2010)	CMW/C/NER/QPR/1
Senegal	Second and third (1 November 2014)	CMW/C/SEN/QPR/2-3

B. Adoption of concluding observations

44. At its twenty-first session, the Committee considered the situation in Belize and the initial report of Ghana in relation to the implementation of the Convention, and adopted concluding observations with respect to both States parties, in accordance with article 74 of the Convention. It should be noted that the situation in Belize was considered in the absence of a report as well as in the absence of a delegation, pursuant to rule 31 bis of its revised provisional rules of procedures (see A/67/48, para. 26).

45. At its twenty-second session, the Committee considered the initial reports of Kyrgyzstan, Peru and Uganda with respect to the implementation of the Convention and adopted concluding observations thereon, in accordance with article 74 of the Convention. The second periodic report of Sri Lanka was scheduled for consideration by the Committee at its twenty-second session, but was postponed at the request of the State party.

46. The concluding observations adopted by the Committee at its twenty-first and twenty-second sessions are available from the Committee's webpage (see www2.ohchr.org) and from the Official Document System of the United Nations (http://documents.un.org) under the symbols indicated below:

State party	Symbol of concluding observations
Belize	CMW/C/BLZ/CO/1
Ghana	CMW/C/GHA/CO/1
Kyrgyzstan	CMW/C/KGZ/CO/1
Peru	CMW/C/PER/CO/1
Uganda	CMW/C/UGA/CO/1

47. Comments and observations by States parties on the concluding observations are available from the Committee's webpage (see www2.ohchr.org) under the relevant session number.

48. A list of documents issued or to be issued in connection with the twenty-first and twenty-second sessions of the Committee is contained in annex IV.

Annex I

States that have signed, ratified or acceded to the International Convention on the Protection of the Rights of All Migrant Workers and Members of Their Families as at 24 April 2015

State	Signature or succession to signature	Ratification, accession or succession
Albania		5 June 2007[a]
Algeria		21 April 2005[a]
Argentina	10 August 2004	23 February 2007
Armenia	26 September 2013	
Azerbaijan		11 January 1999[a]
Bangladesh	7 October 1998	24 August 2011
Belize		14 November 2001[a]
Benin	15 September 2005	
Bolivia (Plurinational State of)		16 October 2000[a]
Bosnia and Herzegovina		13 December 1996[a]
Burkina Faso	16 November 2001	26 November 2003
Cambodia	27 September 2004	
Cameroon	15 December 2009	
Cabo Verde		16 September 1997[a]
Chad	26 September 2012	
Chile	24 September 1993	21 March 2005
Colombia		24 May 1995[a]
Comoros	22 September 2000	
Congo	29 September 2008	
Ecuador		5 February 2002[a]
Egypt		19 February 1993[a]
El Salvador	13 September 2002	14 March 2003
Gabon	15 December 2004	
Ghana	7 September 2000	7 September 2000
Guatemala	7 September 2000	14 March 2003[b]
Guinea		7 September 2000[a]

State	Signature or succession to signature	Ratification, accession or succession
Guinea-Bissau	12 September 2000	
Guyana	15 September 2005	7 July 2010
Haiti	5 December 2013	
Honduras		9 August 2005[a]
Indonesia	22 September 2004	31 May 2012
Jamaica	25 September 2008	25 September 2008
Kyrgyzstan		29 September 2003[a]
Lesotho	24 September 2004	16 September 2005
Liberia	22 September 2004	
Libya		18 June 2004[a]
Madagascar	24 September 2014	
Mali		5 June 2003[a]
Mauritania		22 January 2007[a]
Mexico	22 May 1991	8 March 1999[c]
Montenegro	23 October 2006[d]	
Morocco	15 August 1991	21 June 1993
Mozambique	15 March 2012	19 August 2013
Nicaragua		26 October 2005[a]
Niger		18 March 2009[a]
Nigeria		27 July 2009[a]
Palau	20 September 2011	
Paraguay	13 September 2000	23 September 2008
Peru	22 September 2004	14 September 2005
Philippines	15 November 1993	5 July 1995
Rwanda		15 December 2008[a]
Saint Vincent and the Grenadines		29 October 2010[a]
Sao Tome and Principe	6 September 2000	
Senegal		9 June 1999[a]
Serbia	11 November 2004	
Seychelles		15 December 1994[a]
Sierra Leone	15 September 2000	

State	Signature or succession to signature	Ratification, accession or succession
Sri Lanka		11 March 1996[a]
Syrian Arab Republic		2 June 2005[a]
Tajikistan	7 September 2000	8 January 2002
Timor-Leste		30 January 2004[a]
Togo	15 November 2001	
Turkey	13 January 1999	27 September 2004
Uganda		14 November 1995[a]
Uruguay		15 February 2001[a, e]
Venezuela (Bolivarian Republic of)	4 October 2011	

[a] Accession.

[b] On 11 September 2007, Guatemala made a declaration recognizing the Committee's competence under articles 76 and 77 of the Convention to receive and consider inter-State communications and individual communications, respectively.

[c] On 15 September 2008, Mexico made a declaration recognizing the Committee's competence under article 77 of the Convention to receive individual communications.

[d] Succession to signature.

[e] On 13 April 2012, Uruguay made a declaration recognizing the Committee's competence under article 77 of the Convention to receive individual communications.

Annex II

Membership of the Committee on the Protection of the Rights of All Migrant Workers and Members of Their Families as at 24 April 2015

Name of member	Country of nationality	Term expires on 31 December
José Serrano **Brillantes**	Philippines	2017
Salome **Castellanos Delgado**	Honduras	2017
Pablo **Ceriani Cernadas**	Argentina	2017
Francisco **Carrión Mena**	Ecuador	2015
Fatoumata Abdourhamane **Dicko**	Mali	2017
Ahmed Hassan **El-Borai**	Egypt	2015
Abdelhamid **El-Jamri**	Morocco	2015
Md. Shahidul **Haque**	Bangladesh	2017
Prasad **Kariyawasam**	Sri Lanka	2017
Khedidja **Ladjel**	Algeria	2015
Marco **Nuñez-Melgar Maguiña**	Peru	2015
Germain Zong-Naba **Pimé**	Burkina Faso	2015
Azad **Taghizada**	Azerbaijan	2015
Ahmadou **Tall**	Senegal	2017

Composition of the Bureau

Chair: Francisco **Carrión Mena** (Ecuador)

Vice-Chairs: José Serrano **Brillantes** (Philippines)
Azad **Taghizada** (Azerbaijan)
Ahmadou **Tall** (Senegal)

Rapporteur: Salome **Castellanos Delgado** (Honduras)

Annex III

Submission of reports under article 73 of the Convention as at 24 April 2015

State party	Type of report	Date due	Date report received / date of adoption of List of issues prior to reporting under the simplified reporting procedure	Session at which (will be) examined
Albania	Initial	1 October 2008	6 October 2009	13th session (2010)
	Second	1 November 2015		
Algeria	Initial	1 August 2006	3 June 2008	12th session (2010)
	Second	1 May 2012		
Argentina	Initial	1 June 2008	2 February 2010	15th session (2011)
	Second	1 October 2016		
Azerbaijan	Initial	1 July 2004	22 June 2007	10th session (2009)
	Second	1 May 2011	26 October 2011	18th session (2013)
	Third	1 May 2018		
Bangladesh	Initial	1 December 2012		
Belize[a]	Initial	1 July 2004	List of issues prior to reporting adopted at 18th session (2013)	21st session (2014) in the absence of a report and of a delegation
	Combined initial to third	5 September 2016		
Bolivia (Plurinational State of)	Initial	1 July 2004	22 January 2007	8th session (2008)
	Second	1 July 2009	18 October 2011	18th session (2013)
	Third	1 July 2018		
Bosnia and Herzegovina	Initial	1 July 2004	2 August 2007	10th session (2009)
	Second	1 May 2011	12 August 2011	17th session (2012)
	Third	1 October 2017		
Burkina Faso	Initial	1 March 2005	6 November 2012	19th session (2013)
	Second	13 September 2018		

State party	Type of report	Date due	Date report received / date of adoption of List of issues prior to reporting under the simplified reporting procedure	Session at which (will be) examined
Cabo Verde[a]	Initial	1 July 2004	List of issues prior to reporting adopted at 20th session (2014)	23rd session (2015)
Chile	Initial	1 July 2006	9 February 2010	15th session (2011)
	Second	1 October 2016		
Colombia	Initial	1 July 2004	25 January 2008	10th session (2010)
	Second	1 May 2011	18 October 2011	18th session (2013)
	Third	1 May 2018		
Ecuador[a]	Initial	1 July 2004	27 October 2006	7th session (2007)
	Second	1 July 2009	23 November 2009	13th session (2010)
	Third	1 July 2015		
Egypt	Initial	1 July 2004	6 April 2006	6th session (2007)
	Second	1 July 2009		
El Salvador[a]	Initial	1 July 2004	19 February 2007	9th session (2008)
	Second	1 December 2010	List of issues prior to reporting adopted at 16th session (2012)	20th session (2014)
	Third	1 May 2019		
Ghana[a]	Initial	1 July 2004	List of issues prior to reporting adopted at 18th session (2013)	21st session (2014)
	Follow-up	5 September 2016		
	Second	5 September 2019		
Guatemala	Initial	1 July 2004	8 March 2010	15th session (2011)
	Second	1 October 2016		
Guinea[a]	Initial	1 July 2004	List of issues prior to reporting adopted at 20th session (2014)	23rd session (2015)
Guyana	Initial	1 November 2011		

A/70/48

State party	Type of report	Date due	Date report received / date of adoption of List of issues prior to reporting under the simplified reporting procedure	Session at which (will be) examined
Honduras[a]	Initial	1 December 2006	List of issues prior to reporting adopted at 22nd session (2015)	
Indonesia	Initial	1 September 2013		
Jamaica[a]	Initial	1 January 2010	List of issues prior to reporting to be adopted at 23rd session (2015)	
Kyrgyzstan[a]	Initial	1 January 2005	List of issues prior to reporting adopted at 19th session (2013). Report received on 10 June 2014	22nd session (2015)
	Second			
Lesotho[a]	Initial	1 January 2007	List of issues prior to reporting adopted at 21st session (2014)	24th session (2016)
Libya	Initial	1 October 2005		
Mali[a]	Initial	1 October 2004	29 July 2005	4th session (2006)
	Second	1 October 2009	List of issues prior to reporting adopted at 16th session (2012)	20th session (2014)
	Third	1 May 2019		
Mauritania[a]	Initial	1 May 2008	List of issues prior to reporting adopted at 21st session (2014)	24th session (2016)
Mexico	Initial	1 July 2004	14 November 2005	5th session (2006)
	Second	1 July 2009	9 December 2009	14th session (2011)
	Third	1 April 2016		
Morocco	Initial	1 July 2004	12 July 2012	19th session (2013)
	Second	13 September 2018		
Mozambique	Initial	1 December 2014		

State party	Type of report	Date due	Date report received / date of adoption of List of issues prior to reporting under the simplified reporting procedure	Session at which (will be) examined
Nicaragua[a]	Initial	1 February 2007	List of issues prior to reporting adopted at 22nd session (2015)	
Niger[a]	Initial	1 July 2010	List of issues prior to reporting adopted at 22nd session (2015)	
Nigeria[a]	Initial	1 November 2010	List of issues prior to reporting to be adopted at 23rd session (2015)	
Paraguay	Initial	1 January 2010	10 January 2011	16th session (2012)
	Second	1 May 2017		
Peru	Initial	1 January 2007	14 August 2013	22nd session (2015)
	Second			
Philippines[a]	Initial	1 July 2004	7 March 2008	10th session (2009)
	Second	1 May 2011	List of issues prior to reporting adopted at 16th session (2012)	20th session (2014)
	Third	1 May 2019		
Rwanda	Initial	1 April 2010	21 October 2011	17th session (2012)
	Second	1 October 2017		
Saint Vincent and the Grenadines	Initial	1 February 2012		
Senegal[a]	Initial	1 July 2004	1 December 2009	13th session (2010)
	Second and third	1 November 2014	List of issues prior to reporting adopted at 22nd session (2015)	24th session (2016)
Seychelles[a]	Initial	1 July 2004	List of issues prior to reporting adopted at 20th session (2014)	23rd session (2015)
Sri Lanka[a]	Initial	1 July 2004	23 April 2008	11th session (2009)

State party	Type of report	Date due	Date report received / date of adoption of List of issues prior to reporting under the simplified reporting procedure	Session at which (will be) examined
	Second	1 November 2011	List of issues prior to reporting adopted at 18th session (2013)	25nd session (2016)
Syrian Arab Republic	Initial	1 October 2006	21 December 2006	8th session (2008)
	Second	1 October 2011		
Tajikistan	Initial	1 July 2004	3 December 2010	16th session (2012)
	Second	1 May 2017		
Timor-Leste[a]	Initial	1 May 2005	List of issues prior to reporting adopted at the 20th session (2014)	23rd session (2015)
Turkey[a]	Initial	1 January 2006	List of issues prior to reporting adopted at 20th session (2014)	24th session (2016)
Uganda[a]	Initial	1 July 2004	List of issues prior to reporting adopted at 18th session (2013)	22nd session (2015)
Uruguay	Initial	1 July 2004	30 January 2013	20th session (2014)
	Second	1 May 2019		

a States parties that have either accepted the simplified reporting procedure or with respect to which the Committee decided to review the implementation of the Convention in the absence of a report. In both cases, the lists of issues prior to reporting adopted by the Committee and the written replies to the lists of issues prior to reporting shall be considered as the initial or periodic reports under article 73 (1) (b) of the Convention.

Annex IV

List of documents issued or to be issued in connection with the twenty-first and twenty-second sessions of the Committee

CMW/C/21/1	Provisional annotated agenda and programme of work (twenty-first session)
CMW/C/SR.262-271	Summary records of the twenty-first session
CMW/C/22/1	Provisional annotated agenda and programme of work (twenty-second session)
CMW/C/SR.272-290	Summary records of the twenty-second session
CMW/C/BLZ/QPR/1	List of issues prior to the submission of the initial report of Belize
CMW/C/BLZ/CO/1	Concluding observations of the Committee in the absence of a report: Belize
CMW/C/GHA/QPR/1	List of issues prior to the submission of the initial report of Ghana
CMW/C/GHA/1	Initial report of Ghana under the simplified reporting procedure
CMW/C/GHA/CO/1	Concluding observations of the Committee on the initial report of Ghana
CMW/C/KGZ/QPR/1	List of issues prior to the submission of the initial report of Kyrgyzstan
CMW/C/KGZ/1	Initial report of Kyrgyzstan under the simplified reporting procedure
CMW/C/KGZ/CO/1	Concluding observations of the Committee on the initial report of Kyrgyzstan
CMW/C/PER/1	Initial report of Peru
CMW/C/PER/Q/1	List of issues: Peru
CMW/C/PER/Q/1/Add.1	Written replies from Peru to the list of issues
CMW/C/PER/CO/1	Concluding observations of the Committee on the initial report of Peru
CMW/C/UGA/QPR/1	List of issues prior to the submission of the initial report of Uganda
CMW/C/UGA/1	Initial report of Uganda under the simplified reporting procedure
CMW/C/UGA/CO/1	Concluding observations of the Committee on the initial report of Uganda

GE.15-14039 (E) 210815 160915

Please recycle